GW01606565

Make things Gypsies made

Make things Gypsies made
Marjorie Stapleton
Studio Vista
London

Acknowledgments
The author would like to thank the Hereford and Worcester County Museum for permission to use the photographs on pages 10, 22 and 25; and Miss Mollie Harris of 'The Archers' for her help with claggum. Much of the historical information was gleaned from the *Journals of the Gypsy Law Society* at the University of Liverpool and *Lavengro* by George Borrow (Dent, 1906). Photographs on pages 28, 40, 48, 52 and 60 are by Peter Kibbles.

A Studio Vista book published by
Cassell & Collier Macmillan Publishers Limited,
35 Red Lion Square, London WC1R 4SG
and at Sydney, Auckland, Toronto, Johannesburg
An affiliate of
The Macmillan Publishing Co. Inc.,
New York

First published in 1976

First published in Great Britain 1976

ISBN 0 289 70664 5

Filmset and printed by BAS Printers Limited, Wallop, Hampshire

Contents

Introduction

Smoke behind bushes, gaudy caravans, clothes on the hedge and brown-faced children with rings in their ears all spell 'Gypsies' when seen in the English countryside. Today they prefer to be known as travellers, but their exotic appearance first led people to call them Egyptians – 'Gypsies' for short. They took advantage of this name when hawking, introducing themselves as 'Lords of Little Egypt' to avoid being confused with beggars and tramps.

However, their fascinating Romani language suggests that India was the home they left to wander all over Europe and even as far as America and Australia. First with pack horses and bender tents, later with painted wagons and now in trucks and trailers, they have moved about helping with the harvest, mending kettles and chairs and telling fortunes. They also made and sold a variety of delightful wares to tempt the customer on his own doorstep. As towns have eaten into the countryside and household articles have become factory made, Gypsies have turned to selling scrap for a living and their peculiar arts are almost lost. But before all are forgotten, you might like to make a last wooden chrysanthemum or some lavender bottles, or even tell somebody's fortune – if they cross your palm with silver first.

Chinning the kosht (peg making)

Clothes pegs have been made by Gypsies for longer than anyone can remember. The peg knife, an adapted kitchen knife, is their most useful and versatile tool. They even take out teeth with it. Peg making, known in Romani language as chinning the kosht, has always been the man's job. A group of two or three men working together could turn out a gross in an hour. The women sold the pegs from door to door. In addition to the large hawking basket, many carried their chavies, or children, in shawls tied across their shoulders. They covered miles like this, often in heavy old hobnailed boots.

Selling their wares has never been easy for Gypsy women. Country folk believed them to have the 'power of the eye' and feared them. They also were convinced that Gypsies stole children and made sure their infants could chant the old clapping rhyme:

My mother said that I never should
Play with the Gypsies in the wood.

But it is highly unlikely that any Gypsy would have stolen a child: they had more than enough of their own.

To make pegs you need:

either an old kitchen knife and short screwdriver handle to make a peg knife

or a penknife

a piece of hard wood such as beech 30 × 13 cm (or 12 × 5 in) for an anvil

a second piece of hard wood 30 × 7 cm (or 12 × $2\frac{1}{2}$ in) for a hammer

an old biscuit tin

pincers

thin straight branches from a hedge (Hazel and willow are best. They should not be too green and sappy, nor too dead and brittle, and they should be as thick as a man's finger, with no knots in them.)

Gypsy peg knife
Break the blade out of the handle of the old kitchen knife. You will find that it is mounted on a pin. Fix this into the handle of an old stubby bradawl or screwdriver handle. Grind the blade on a grindstone until it is 9 cm (or $3\frac{1}{2}$ in) long, with a sharp edge and a rounded end.

Anvil and hammer
Cut the base of the thicker piece of hard wood into a point that will stick firmly into the ground. The other piece of wood will act as the hammer.

Making the pegs
Hammer the anvil into the ground and sit comfortably in front of it with the bundle of branches by your side and the peg knife in your left hand. Bend up your left knee and hook your left arm round it, holding the knife firmly against your knee.

Take a branch in your right hand and pull it towards you, turning it against the sharp edge of the blade until you have stripped off all the bark. This is known as chinning.

Chin the rest of the branches in the same way.

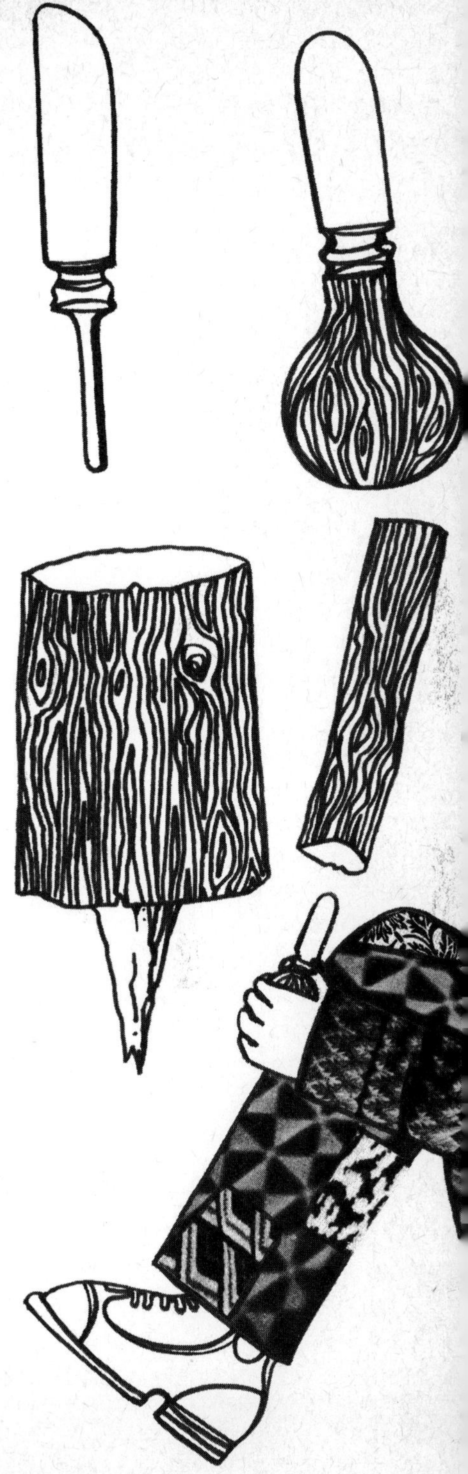

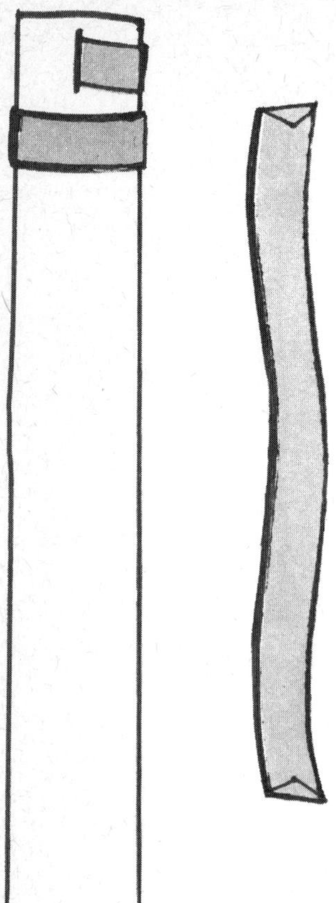

Lay a stripped branch on the anvil and hold the knife across it. Cut it up into koshtis 13 cm (or 5 in) long by tapping the knife with the hammer. Cut up the other stripped branches in the same way.

Put the chinned koshtis in the sun for an hour to shrink slightly before tinning.

Place the old biscuit tin on the ground, pull it apart, and beat it out flat with your hammer. With the pincers tear it into strips about 50 mm (or $\frac{1}{4}$ in) wide and 20 cm (or 8 in) long. Hammer them flat and bend a corner down at each end of each strip to make a point.

Hammer one of the pointed ends of a strip into the top of a koshti. Wind the strip round the koshti two or three times and secure it by hammering in the other turned down corner.

Tin the other koshtis in the same way. Sometimes, as an alternative, small brads were hammered in to attach the metal strip.

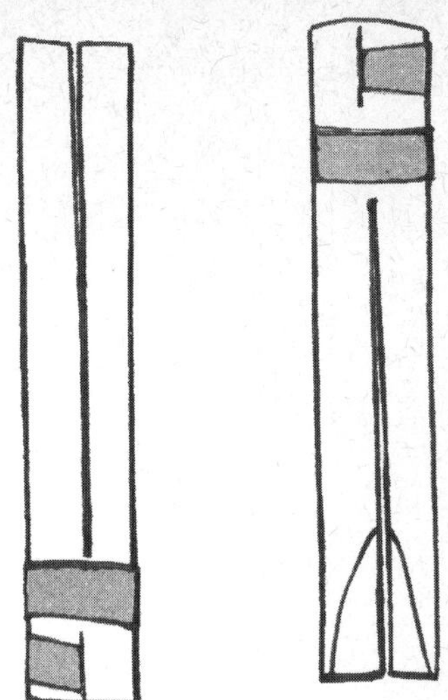

Holding each koshti on the anvil in turn, split the wood as far as the tin with the peg knife.

Pare the bottom end by making two curved cuts as shown in the drawing.

Mouth the peg by making two clean cuts. Push the peg knife, blunt side uppermost, up the split as far as the tin. Then make a clean cut down and out to the bottom. Push the knife backwards up the split again and cut down the other side in the same way.

Now your peg has smooth rounded tapered ends that will not tear the clothes.

Twenty or so koshtis were pegged on a twig in alternate directions as a convenient way of presenting them for sale.

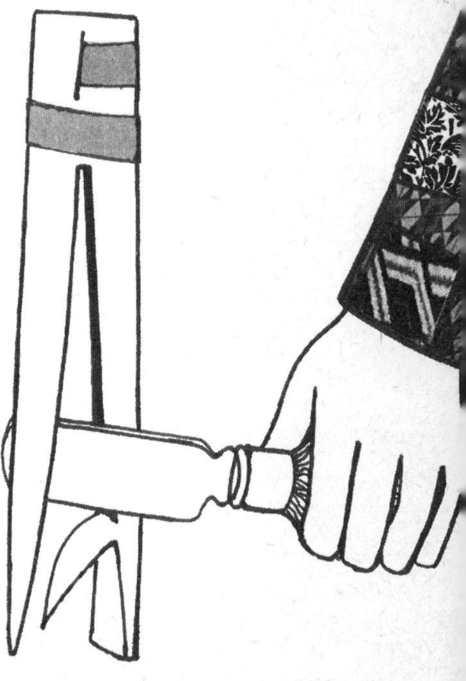

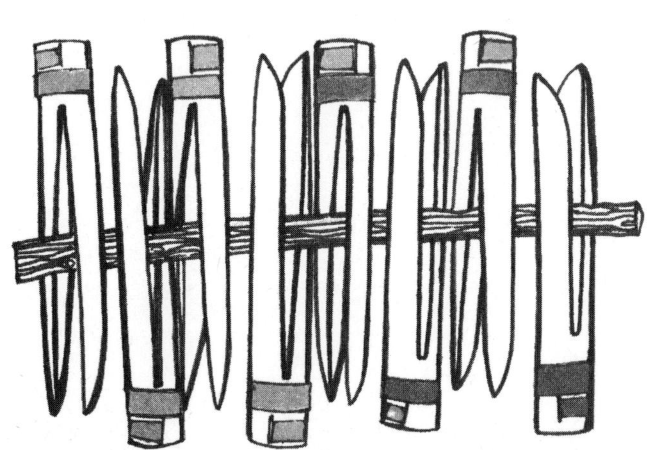

Joddakai (apron)

Gypsy women could put on the contents of a ragbag and look like royalty. In days gone by they liked to wear layers of multi-coloured cast-off skirts with coins sewn onto them. These coins and their jangling jewelry were no cheap fakes; they were real silver and gold. Valuables could not be left in tents and wagons, so the family fortune was worn by the wife. Old clothes were collected on doorsteps and rag sorting was full of excitement. Desirable dresses were often torn in two in the fight. Soft pieces were saved for toe rags to keep feet warm in winter and ease the pain of walking for miles in other people's boots.

The men liked a flashy belt, moleskin jacket and a bright diklo – the little scarf wound twice round the neck and knotted.

Both sexes were fond of dressing in bits of old military uniforms and neither were often without their beloved sweggler s – the little curved pipes in which they smoked anything from shredded oak leaves to coltsfoot.

The one garment women took the trouble to make or have made was the spectacular joddakai, an apron worn sixty years ago on special occasions such as flowerselling, fortune telling or minding coconut shies at country fairs. It was made from black Italian cloth, tucked and embroidered in vivid silks and often finished with black crochet work.

To make a Gypsy apron you need:
1.60 m (or $1\frac{3}{4}$ yd) of 90 cm (36 in) wide black silky material
black sewing silk
tacking cotton
cherry red embroidery silk
odd lengths of vividly coloured embroidery silk
a warm iron
pins, scissors and a piece of tailor's chalk

This apron measures 56 cm (22 in) from waist to hem, but can easily be cut longer or shorter if you wish.

Fold the material in half. Using the ruler and tailor's chalk mark it out as shown below. Pin along the insides of the chalk lines and cut out the six pieces.

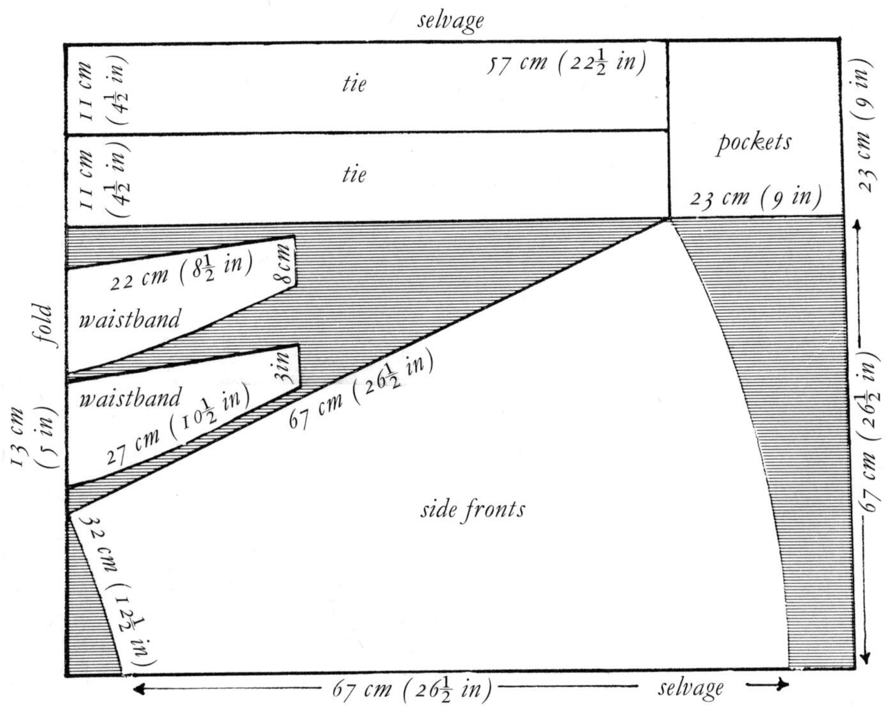

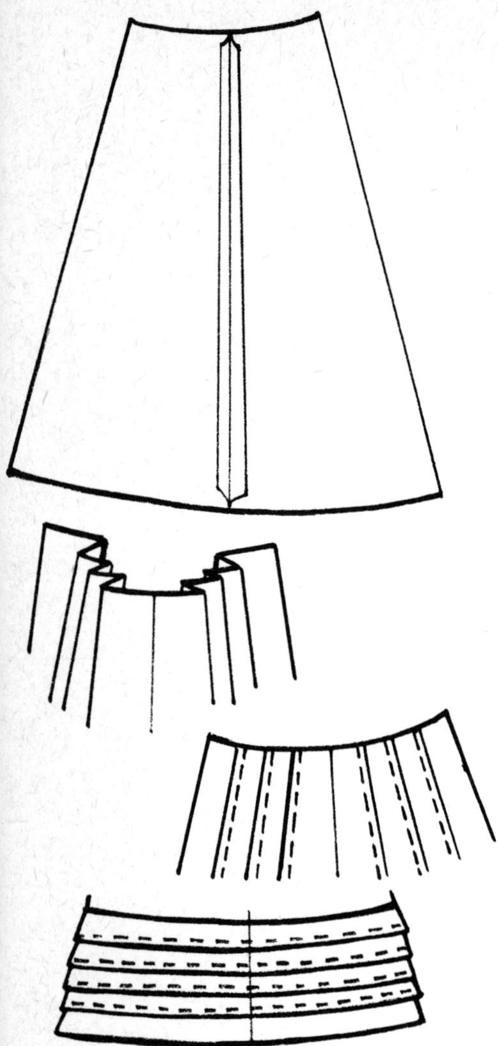

Sew the fronts together, right sides facing, along the selvage. Press the seam open. These two together form the front of the apron.

Make three 1.25 cm (or ½ in) tucks along the top edge, each side of the central seam. Pin and tack each one down to a depth of 13 cm (or 5 in). With the right side facing, sew along the edge of each tuck to form six raised pleats.

Pin and sew five 1.25 cm (or ½ in) tucks across the apron in the same way. The first one should be 38 cm (15 in) from the top and the last one 14 cm (5½ in) from the bottom. The other three should be closely spaced between them.

Hem neatly round the sides and bottom of the apron.

Turn under the long 'V'-shaped edges of the two waist bands about 1 cm (⅜ in). Tack down the turnings and press them. With the right sides together, sew the two waistband pieces together along the curved edge. Turn the waistband the right side out and press it.

Tack the apron front between the turned under 'V'-shaped edges of the waistband. With the right side of the apron uppermost, stitch along the lower edge of the waistband.

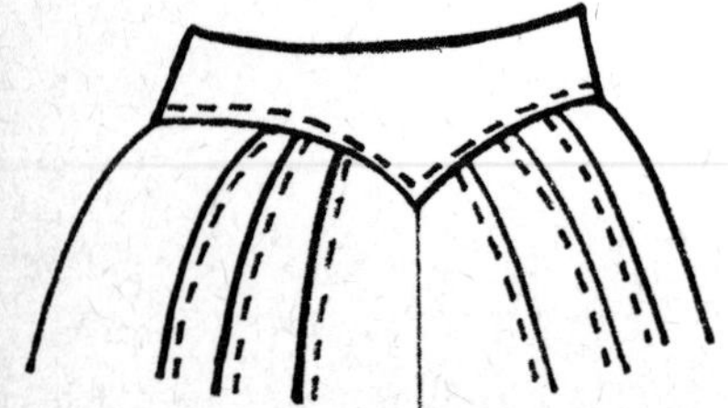

Fold the two long ties lengthways, right sides together. Sew along the long side and one short side. Turn the ties right side out and press them.

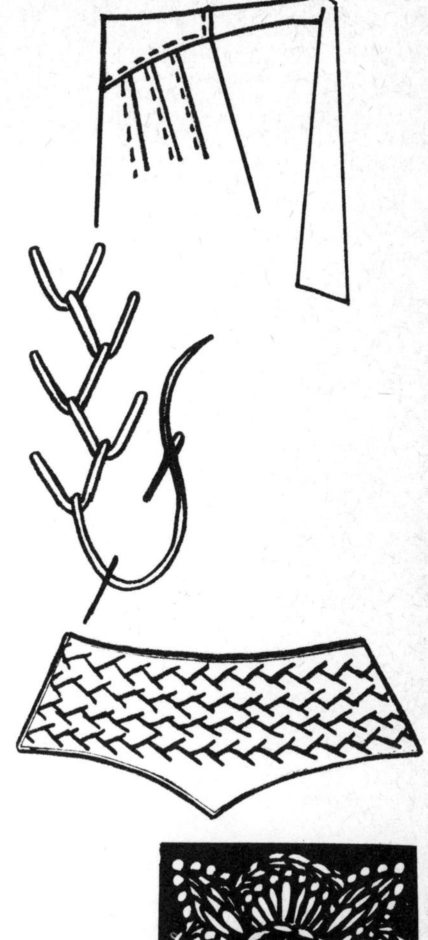

Insert the unstitched ends of the ties into the open ends of the waistband. Turn in the waistband edges and stitch through on the outside to attach the ties.

Turn in and tack the edges of the last two squares to make pockets. Make sure that they are the right size to fit between the top and bottom raised tucks on the apron front. Do not attach them yet.

Cover the waistband with bold featherstitching in cherry red silk (see diagrams). Now, using multicoloured silks, embroider a large flamboyant flower on each square. Cover the whole pocket area, making the flowers as vivid and inventive as you can. The drawings may give you some ideas.

When both flowers are completed, press the squares under a damp cloth and sew them onto the apron. Border each pocket with red featherstitching.

Some aprons had a border of black crochet added to the hem; others had the apron front gathered onto the waistband with coloured smocking stitches.

Wooden Chrysanthemums

The painted Gypsy wagons, or vardos, were homes rather than vehicles. Only the very old and the very young were allowed to ride. The rest walked to save the horse. Most of the vardos had a comfortable bed across the back with a drawer underneath for children to sleep in. As the family increased older members slept outside in drooping arrangements of sacks, carpets and hazel boughs called bender tents. A good vardo had fitted cupboards with mirrors and cut glass knobs, and tasselled and bobbled cushions and curtains, and some even boasted Crown Derby china. In contrast to the often squalid camp site the vardo was a showpiece.

Achin-tans, or camping grounds, are hard to find and Gypsies still make patrins, their secret signs, to pass on information about them to each other. A hazel twig standing in the ground with two strips of bark hanging from it means the site is no good. A similar one with one side bared shows the way the vardos have gone and thereafter clods of earth are placed at crossroads to mark the trail. Crossed twigs with one sharpened end indicate a good site.

Once the Gypsies had camped and lit the fire, work started again. Often wooden chrysanthemum heads were made as a change from koshtis. The men skilfully fashioned them with a peg knife and the women dyed them improbable colours and mounted them on evergreen sprays ready to sell.

To make wooden chrysanthemums you need:

straight twigs, cut from a hedge, at least as thick as a man's finger and about 25 cm (or 10 in) long (Elder, hazel and willow are all suitable. They should be straight and sappy rather than brittle)
a sharp peg knife (see page 11) or penknife
a peg anvil (see page 11)
coloured dye or ink
a nail
evergreen sprays

Pare off the bark from the twigs in the same way as in pegmaking (see page 11). Chop up the stripped branches into 25 cm (or 10 in) sticks on a peg anvil.

Hold the end of one of the sticks in your left hand with its base standing firmly on the anvil. Shave a strip away from it. Start just below your left hand and stop a short distance from the base, leaving the bottom end of the strip attached to the stick. It will form a frond curling back from the stick.

Shave another strip beside it. Gradually turn the stick and shave more strips until you have a ring of curled fronds.

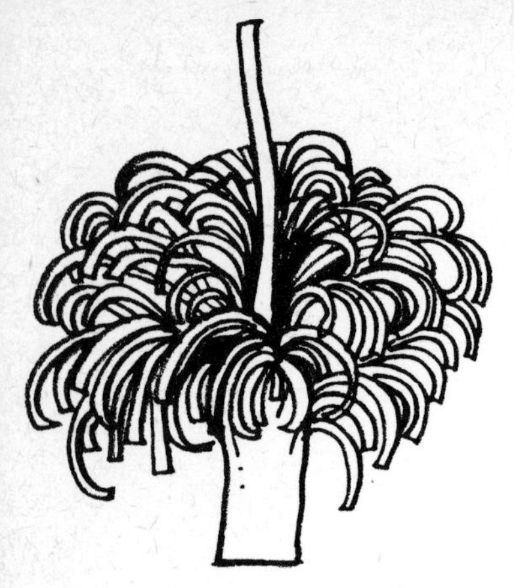

Cut a second ring of fine fronds above the first one.

Rotating the stick base on the anvil, cut rings of fronds until you have shaved the whole of the twig away and the part in your hand drops off leaving a wooden chrysanthemum head.

Make some more flower heads in the same way.

Prepare pans or bowls of dye. Household dye, coloured inks or food dyes mixed with water would all be suitable. The Gypsies made dye by boiling rags in the days when fabric dyes were not colour fast. They favoured pink and orange, but the chrysanthemums were made in every colour imaginable.

Dip the flower heads into the dye for a few minutes then spread them out to dry out of doors or on some old newspaper.

When they are dry, poke out the pith in the base of each one with an old nail to make a hole for the stem.

Mount the heads on sprays of evergreen leaves and they will be ready to give away or take out bikknin, the Gypsy name for hawking.

This brush was made from one stick in the same way as the chrysanthemums. Gypsies made these brushes to sell, and also used them to dust out their wagons.

To make one you need: patience, a very sharp knife, and a steady hand and eye to cut the fronds so finely that they twist and curl. Experiment with different twigs, as some woods will twist more readily than others.

Cut your stick at least 38 cm (15 in) long and hold it on the peg anvil in the same way as the chrysanthemum stick.

Pare the strips from below your left hand, but this time leave the base 20 cm (8 in) long as it will form the handle of the brush.

Work neatly and skilfully in the same way as before until the brush head is complete.

You could add a pretty spiral pattern to the handle.

Grip the lower end of the brush handle in your left hand, hold the brush head between your knees, and gently scrape the fronds from the upper handle in the same way as before.

Manacles, honeyballs and claggum

The centre of Gypsy life is still the camp fire or yog. Only people who live out of doors know its true value. You may never pass between a Gypsy and his yog and must know him for seven years before you venture to poke it.

At Rommerins, Gypsy weddings, the yog featured in the ceremony. The bride and groom were each given a slight cut on the wrist with a peg knife. Their wrists were bound and then they jumped over the yog to show that they were even prepared to go through fire together. A wedding feast simmered on adjacent yogs. Favourite dishes were hotchi-witchi (hedgehog baked in clay and said to taste like tender roast pork) and Gypsy stew made from potatoes, carrots, turnips and nettles with pheasant, hare, pigeon or rabbit. The banqueting area was decorated with buckets of furze, the Gypsy flower, and guests brought their own cutlery and mugs.

Among the most delicious of Gypsy fried fare are the large, spicy Welsh cakes called manacles, and honeyballs made from batter. In the old days Gypsy women made claggum, a kind of toffee, to sell at fairs to Gaujos – their name for us, and also for barbarians.

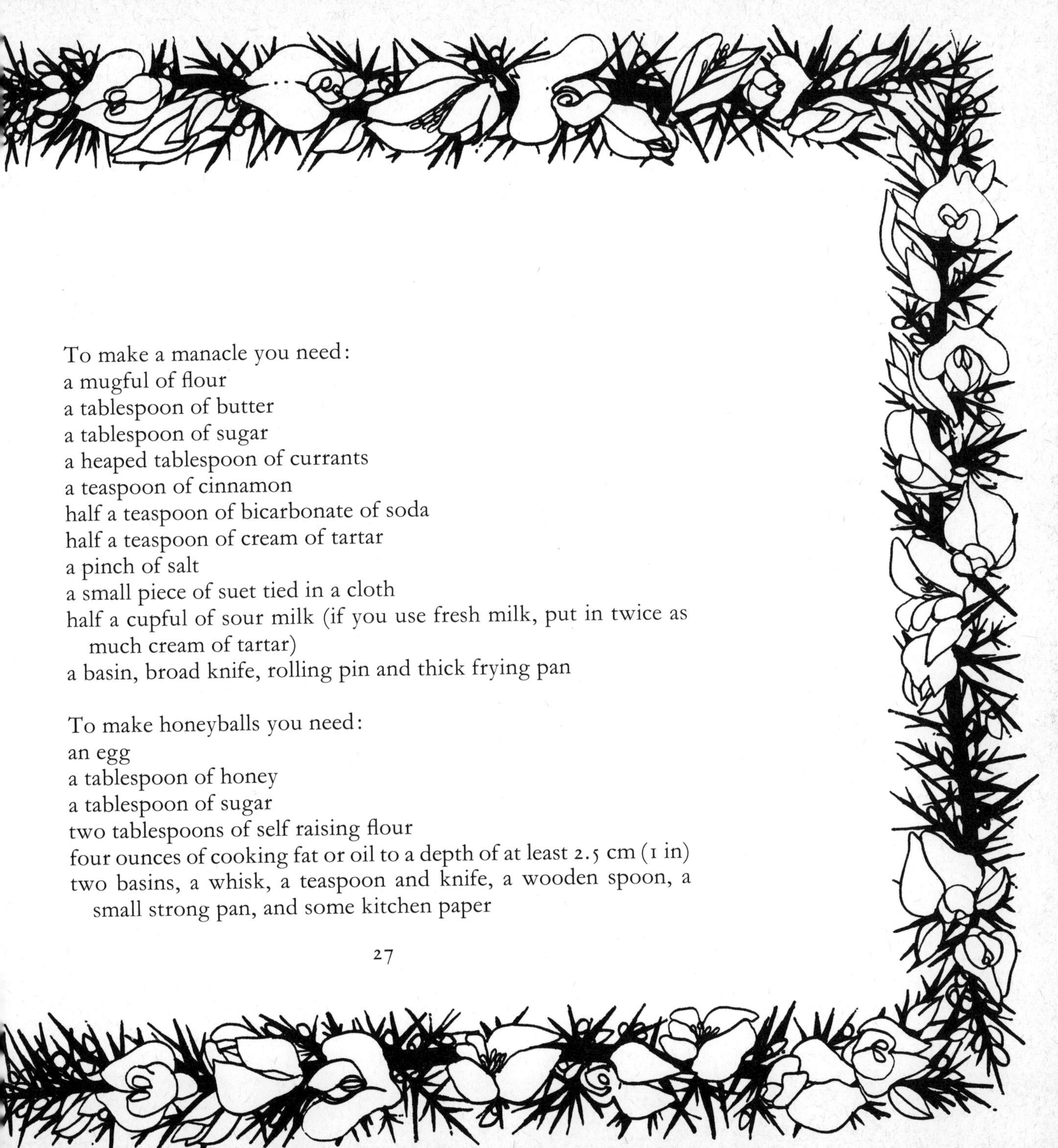

To make a manacle you need:
a mugful of flour
a tablespoon of butter
a tablespoon of sugar
a heaped tablespoon of currants
a teaspoon of cinnamon
half a teaspoon of bicarbonate of soda
half a teaspoon of cream of tartar
a pinch of salt
a small piece of suet tied in a cloth
half a cupful of sour milk (if you use fresh milk, put in twice as much cream of tartar)
a basin, broad knife, rolling pin and thick frying pan

To make honeyballs you need:
an egg
a tablespoon of honey
a tablespoon of sugar
two tablespoons of self raising flour
four ounces of cooking fat or oil to a depth of at least 2.5 cm (1 in)
two basins, a whisk, a teaspoon and knife, a wooden spoon, a small strong pan, and some kitchen paper

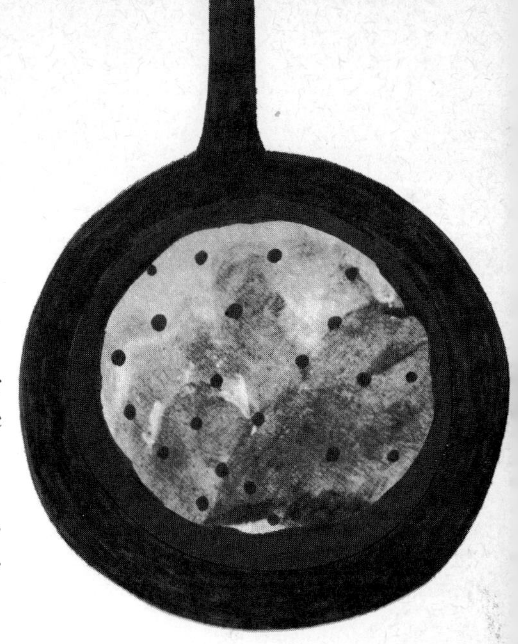

Manacle
Put the flour and butter into the basin and rub them together.

Add all the other ingredients (except the milk and suet) and stir them together with the knife. Stir in enough sour milk to make a light dough.

Take the rolling pin and lightly roll the dough into a large circle. It should be about 2.5 cm (or 1 in) thick and fit the frying pan. Try to handle it as little as possible.

Heat up the frying pan and rub the cotton bag of suet all over the bottom until it is well greased. Lift the dough carefully into the pan and cook it for about six minutes on each side until it is dry, crisp and golden.

Slide the knife under the manacle to remove it from the pan. Serve it cut up in buttered slices.

Honeyballs
Separate the white and yoke of the egg. Whisk up the white until it is very stiff.

Add the sugar and honey to the yolk and beat them together with the wooden spoon until the mixture is pale and creamy.

Sprinkle the flour into the mixture and then lightly fold in the egg white.

Heat up the fat or oil in the pan until it shows signs of hazing but not smoking. If it smokes, it is too hot: leave it to cool for a few minutes.

Holding the teaspoon in the right hand and the knife in the left, drop one teaspoonful of the mixture at a time into the hot fat. It will swell into a honeyball the size of a walnut and the under side will turn golden brown in a few seconds. Flip it over carefully with the knife and spoon to brown the top side, then lift it out on the kitchen paper.

Make the rest in the same way. If the fat starts smoking remove the pan from the heat for a few minutes. But be careful not to let it grow too cool or the honeyballs will be greasy.

Hand them round and eat them immediately.

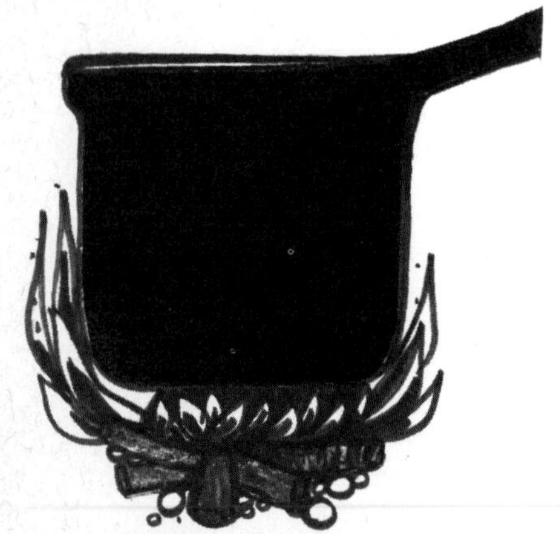

Claggum rock

Gypsy women crouched for hours round their cooking pots stirring treacle and brown sugar into claggum or fair rock to hawk round the fairs at a penny a lump. After cooking it they would tip it onto a board, spit on their hands and throw it onto a hook on the side of the wagon. Here they pulled it to the right length before cutting it up.

To make claggum you need:

a mugful of treacle
a mugful of brown sugar
a tablespoon of butter
a dessertspoon of vinegar
half a teaspoon of bicarbonate of soda
a large heavy pan, a wooden spoon, a greased oven tin, a greased board, kitchen scissors or a peg knife, two cups, and a convenient firm hook such as a cup hook on a kitchen shelf

Put the treacle, sugar, butter and vinegar into the pan and slowly bring them to the boil, stirring with the wooden spoon. Have a cup of cold water handy and drop a few drips of toffee into it at regular intervals. When it hardens as soon as it touches the water the claggum is ready to pull.

Take the pan off the heat and add the bicarbonate of soda dissolved in a drop of hot water in the other cup. Pour the toffee into the greased oven tin and push it to the middle with the spoon.

As soon as it is cool enough to handle, pick it up and slap it onto the hook. Pull it until it looks white. Now put it on the greased board and, losing no time, cut it up into lumps with the scissors or peg knife.

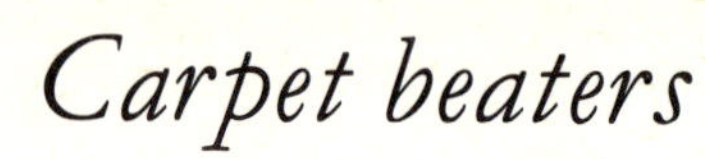

Carpet beaters

Gypsy names are often very unusual. There are old Romani names such as Mizella and Ryella or surprisingly original ones like Liberty, Freedom, Britannia, Comfort, Crimea and Hemlock. Cinderella is also a favourite. Gypsies are given two Christian names, the first of which is kept secret. A Gypsy baby is traditionally born on straw and at the moment of birth his mother whispers his secret name. This is never used but whispered to him again on his coming of age. Gypsies believe that no one can harm them with evil spells if their true identity is kept a secret known only to close relatives.

Family groups are closely knit and these gregarious people were sometimes ruled over by their numerous Gypsy kings and queens. Making carpet beaters was a family craft, each family working its own characteristic pattern and swearing that theirs was 'the bestest at whamming out the muck'. The very attractive designs included 'farmhouse twist', 'butterfly', 'sunflower',

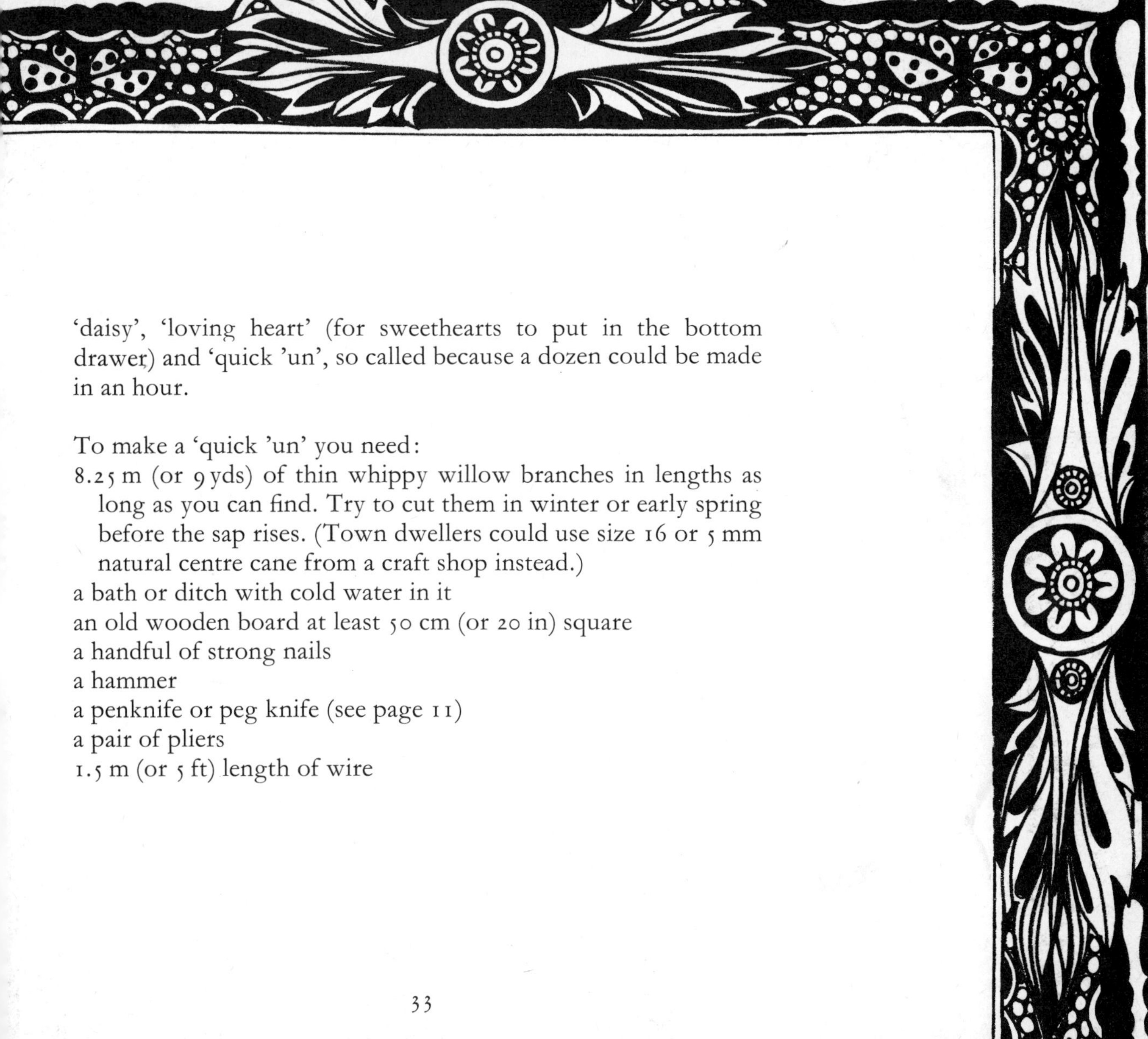

'daisy', 'loving heart' (for sweethearts to put in the bottom drawer) and 'quick 'un', so called because a dozen could be made in an hour.

To make a 'quick 'un' you need:

8.25 m (or 9 yds) of thin whippy willow branches in lengths as long as you can find. Try to cut them in winter or early spring before the sap rises. (Town dwellers could use size 16 or 5 mm natural centre cane from a craft shop instead.)
a bath or ditch with cold water in it
an old wooden board at least 50 cm (or 20 in) square
a handful of strong nails
a hammer
a penknife or peg knife (see page 11)
a pair of pliers
1.5 m (or 5 ft) length of wire

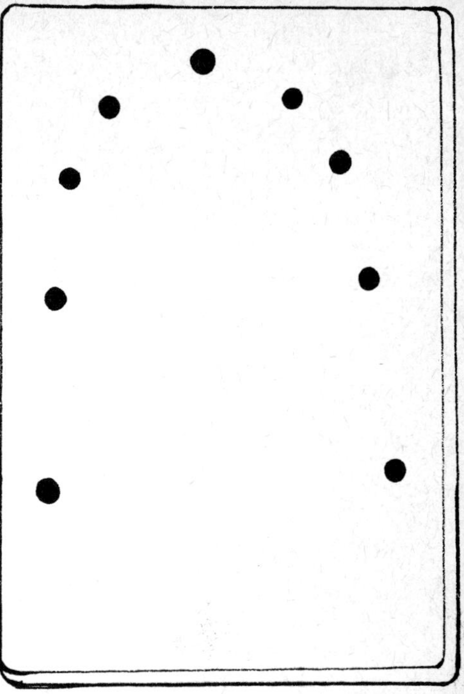

Soak the willow branches in a bath or, like the Gypsies, in a ditch of cold water for five days.

Take them out and lay them in a sheltered place to mellow for a night.

Hammer a large nail into the centre top of the board leaving it sticking out 2.5 cm (or 1 in). This is known as the big pin.

Hammer in the other nails as shown in the drawing. Leave them sticking out the same amount.

Prop up the board on a table with a log or a few books so that it slopes gently towards you as you stand before it to work. The board was called a slap and making carpet beaters was known as wrapping. The Gypsy always stood to wrap, usually resting his slap on the food basket rack on the back of the wagon.

Take a long branch of willow and, holding it like a skipping rope, bend it round the big pin in a curve.

Using both hands together, start wrapping under and over, round the nails in the pattern shown in the drawing.

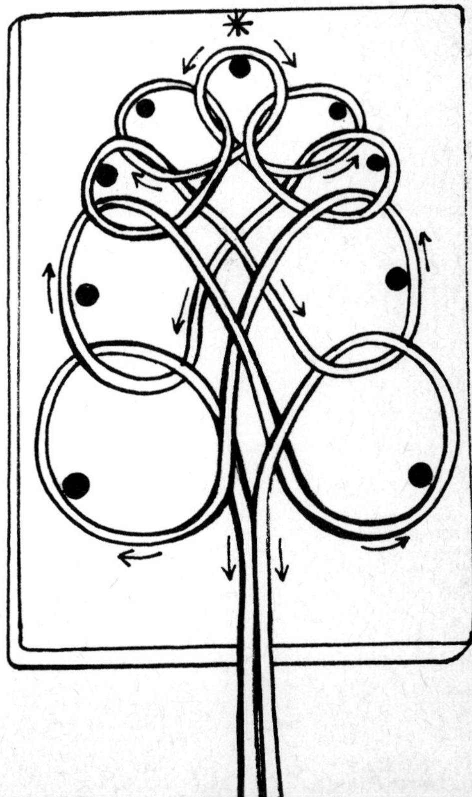

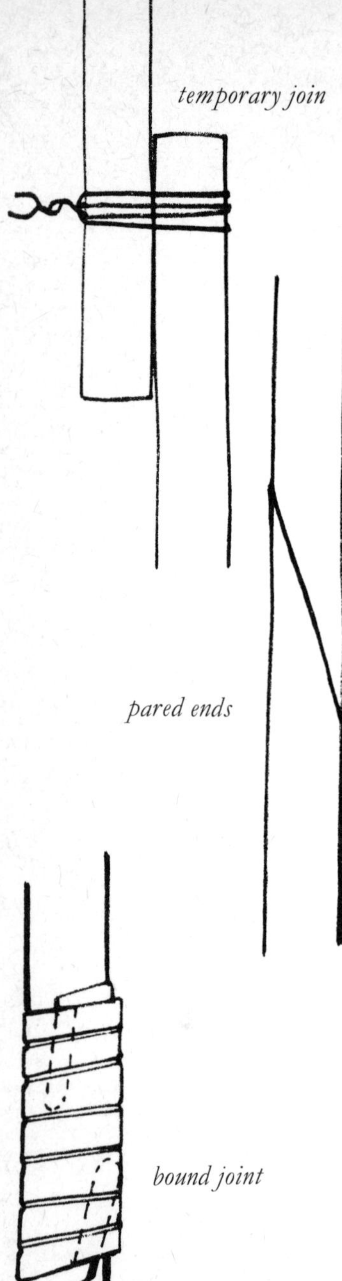

Where you have to join on new lengths of willow, overlap them 5 cm (2 in) and hold the two ends together temporarily with a twist of wire.

When you reach the bottom of the design, leave two lengths hanging down to form the handle. Join these temporarily top and bottom, with twists of wire.

Use the knife to strip the remaining willow branches into thin skeins. Untie the wires, one at a time, and pare the willow ends to fit neatly together as shown in the picture. Apply a little glue to them if you wish.

Bind the joints firmly with a skein of willow, threading the ends underneath the binding.

Bind and finish the handle in the same way.

Once you have mastered 'quick 'un' you might like to try 'butterfly' and 'loving heart', made in the same way, or 'sunflower' and 'farmhouse twist' made with one hand only. Experienced wrappers made these with their other hand in their pocket.

'Loving heart', sold to girls for their bottom drawer, was the oldest design of all. 'Them you can see in the middle, pretty lady, is two loving sweethearts twined together to bring you a happy marriage.'

start at the points
marked with a star
butterfly
loving heart
farmhouse twist
sunflower

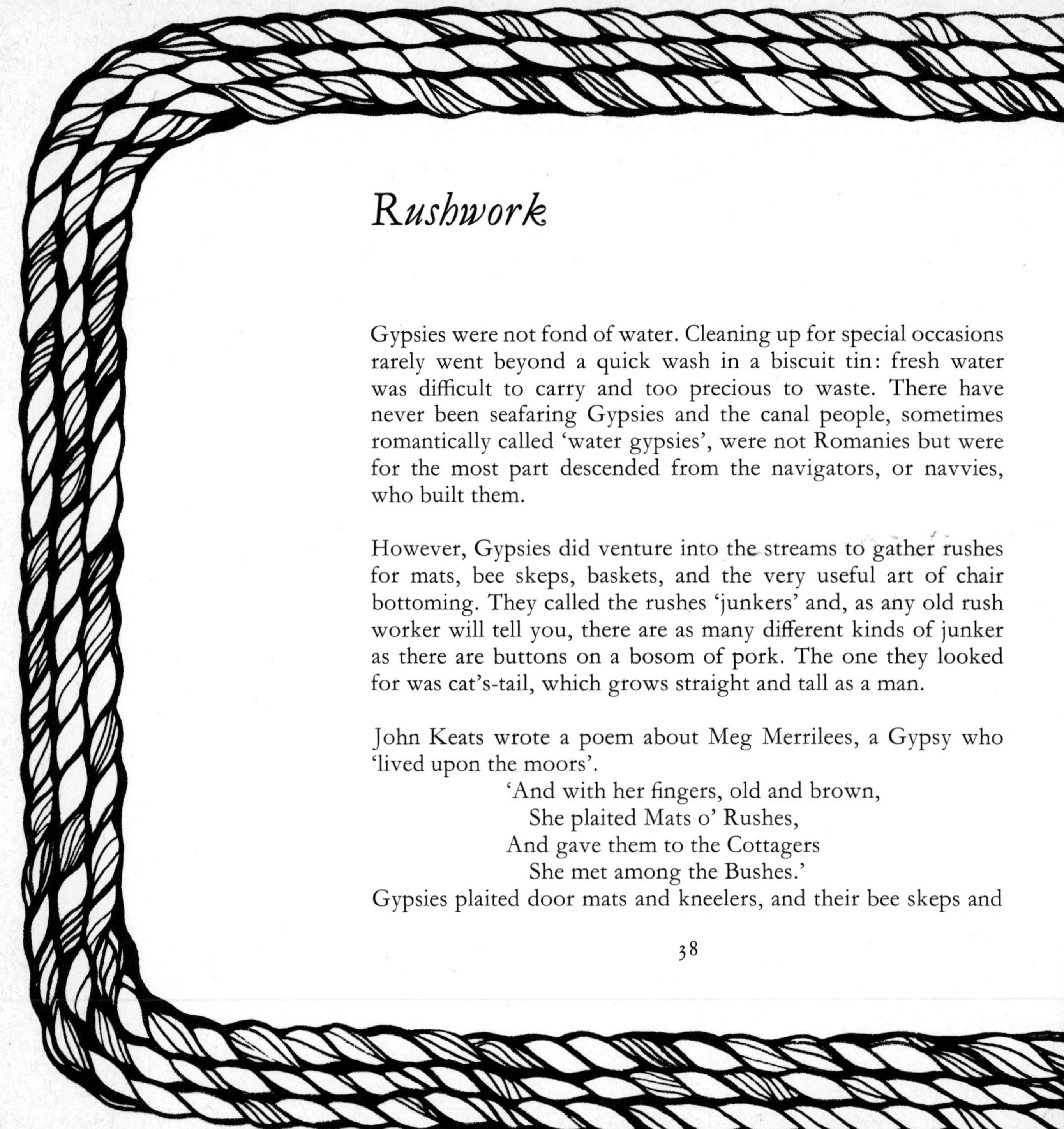

Rushwork

Gypsies were not fond of water. Cleaning up for special occasions rarely went beyond a quick wash in a biscuit tin: fresh water was difficult to carry and too precious to waste. There have never been seafaring Gypsies and the canal people, sometimes romantically called 'water gypsies', were not Romanies but were for the most part descended from the navigators, or navvies, who built them.

However, Gypsies did venture into the streams to gather rushes for mats, bee skeps, baskets, and the very useful art of chair bottoming. They called the rushes 'junkers' and, as any old rush worker will tell you, there are as many different kinds of junker as there are buttons on a bosom of pork. The one they looked for was cat's-tail, which grows straight and tall as a man.

John Keats wrote a poem about Meg Merrilees, a Gypsy who 'lived upon the moors'.

'And with her fingers, old and brown,
She plaited Mats o' Rushes,
And gave them to the Cottagers
She met among the Bushes.'

Gypsies plaited door mats and kneelers, and their bee skeps and

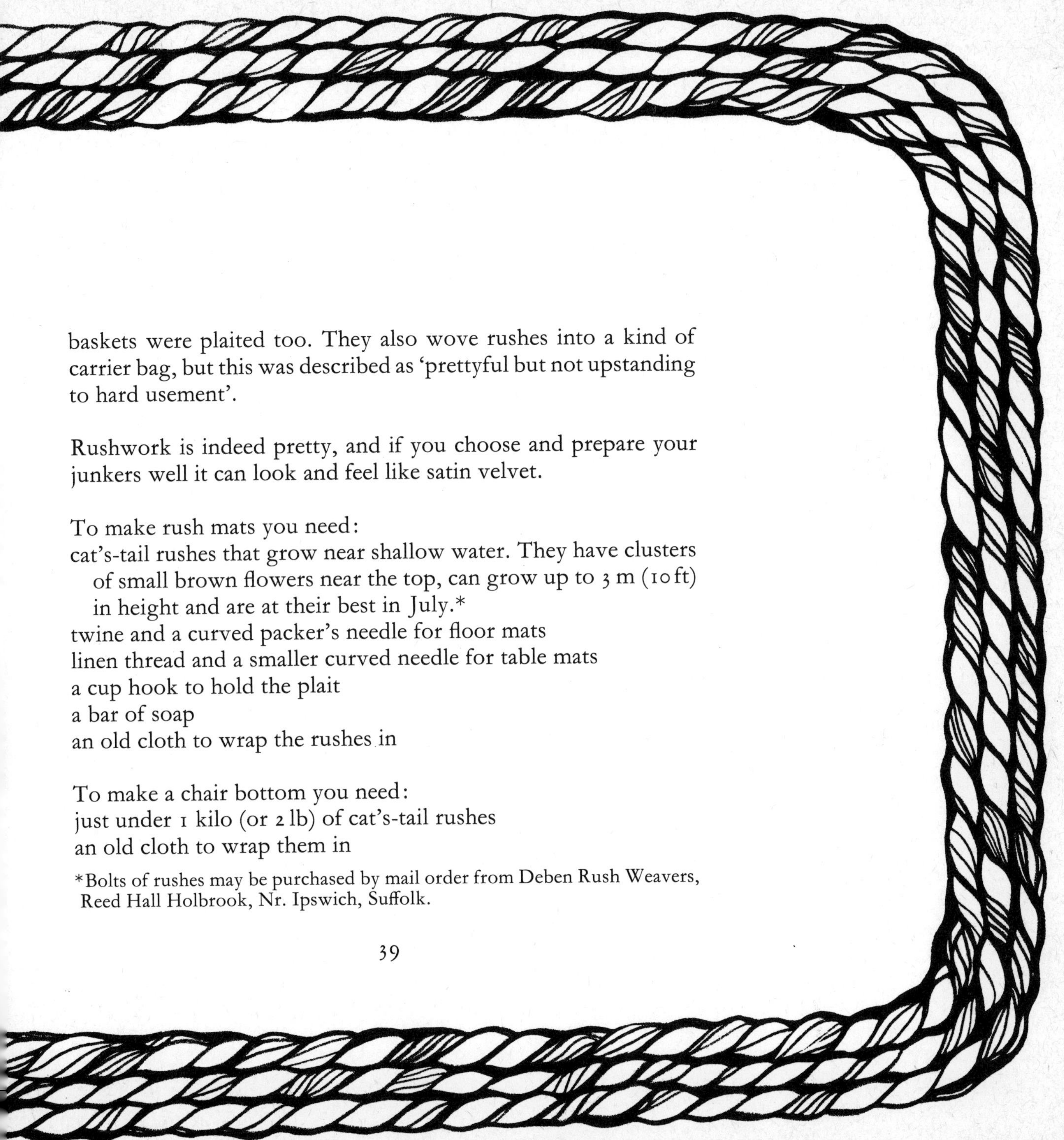

baskets were plaited too. They also wove rushes into a kind of carrier bag, but this was described as 'prettyful but not upstanding to hard usement'.

Rushwork is indeed pretty, and if you choose and prepare your junkers well it can look and feel like satin velvet.

To make rush mats you need:
cat's-tail rushes that grow near shallow water. They have clusters of small brown flowers near the top, can grow up to 3 m (10 ft) in height and are at their best in July.*
twine and a curved packer's needle for floor mats
linen thread and a smaller curved needle for table mats
a cup hook to hold the plait
a bar of soap
an old cloth to wrap the rushes in

To make a chair bottom you need:
just under 1 kilo (or 2 lb) of cat's-tail rushes
an old cloth to wrap them in

*Bolts of rushes may be purchased by mail order from Deben Rush Weavers, Reed Hall Holbrook, Nr. Ipswich, Suffolk.

Gather the cat's-tail rushes in July and spread them out to dry for a week or so in the open air or in a dry airy place. Turn them over occasionally. When they are quite dry they can be stored without risk of rotting. Tie them in a bundle (a bundle of rushes is called a bolt) and store it in a dry place.

When you wish to use some rushes, take them from the bolt and make them pliable again by soaking them for ten minutes in a bath of cold water. The Gypsies soaked them in a ditch.

Wrap the softened rushes in a damp cloth, leaving them to mellow in it for a day and a night. They are now ready to use.

To make a table mat, screw the cup hook into a wall or post at a comfortable height for plaiting work.

Take three long rushes of equal thickness and tie the thick ends together with linen thread. Hang the tied bunch on the hook.

Evenly plait the rushes, left over middle, right over middle.

Join in new ones as they are needed, by placing the thick end of the new length alongside the tapering end of the old one and plaiting with both together three or four times.

Continue plaiting with the new length, leaving the old end protruding through the back to be cut off later.

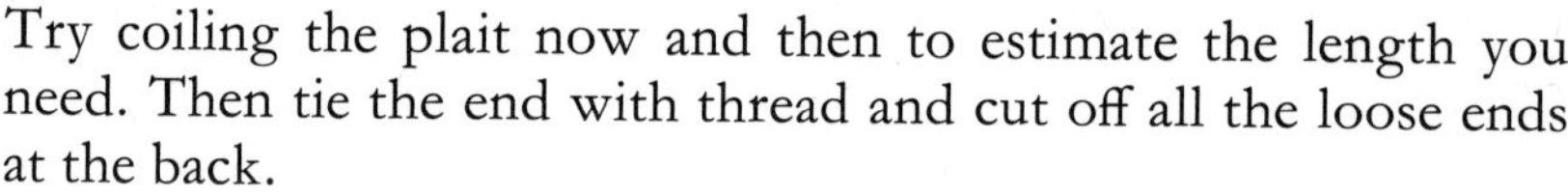

Try coiling the plait now and then to estimate the length you need. Then tie the end with thread and cut off all the loose ends at the back.

Coil the mat, sewing it together with linen thread as you go. Prod the needle into a bar of soap now and then to make it slip more easily through the rushes. On the final round, try to hide the stitches behind the folds of the plait. Finish off by sliding the three rush ends into a fold in the plait on the previous round and secure them with a stitch.

Floor and kneeling mats are made in the same way. Plait them with two or three rushes to each strand to make a thicker mat. Sew the plaits together with twine, again using soap to make the sewing easier. You can make up your own attractive designs by stitching different arrangements of coils together.

Kneelers, useful when scrubbing and polishing floors, can have carrying handles made by leaving loops free when sewing round the final rim.

Basket

To make a basket, plait together three bunches of seven or eight rushes, twisting each bunch half a turn in the same direction each time you bring it over to plait it in.

Sew the base of the basket with twine in the same way as a mat,

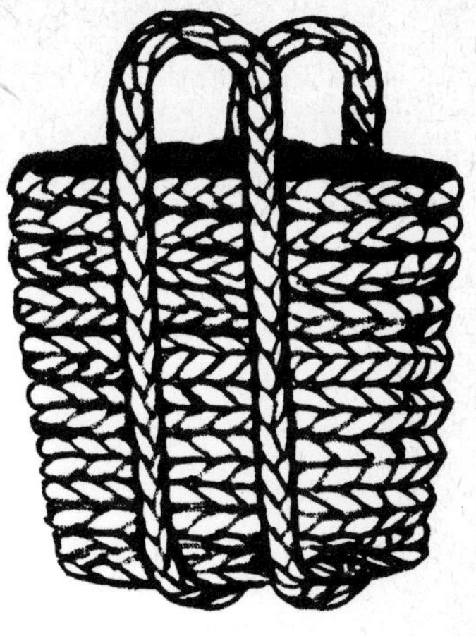

then change direction to build up the sides.

Finish off the top rim by undoing the last few inches of the plait. Damp the end with water and then re-plait it, gradually tapering it by leaving rush ends protruding through the back until only three remain. Tie the end and cut off the stragglers at the back. Sew the end down, tucking the last three tails into the folds of the plait below.

Make one long plait and sew it onto the basket to form two carrying loops joined together under the base.

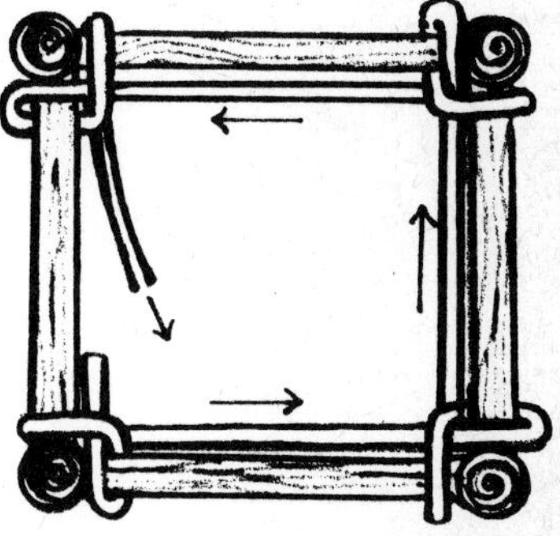

Chair seat
A new rush seat for a chair looks impressive but is surprisingly easy to make. You need 600 grammes (or $1\frac{1}{4}$ lb) of rushes prepared as for the mat.

Tie the thick ends of two rushes together and twist them to make a tough strand. Twist and knot the strand into the chair frame as shown in the drawing. Tie on new rushes as you need them. Use reef knots and tuck the tails to the inside.

Wrap and knot the strand round again and again, working towards the centre. As pockets form between the two layers, stuff them with broken rushes to make a firm seat. Finish off on the wrong side by knotting the left-over length to the rush next to it and threading the loose end into the seat.

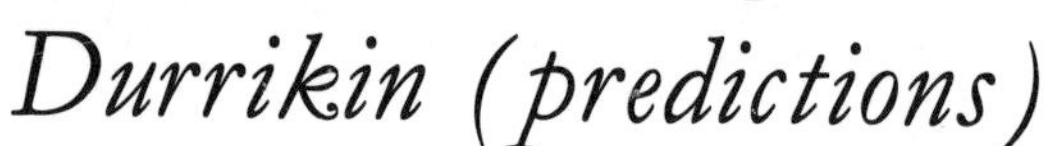

Durrikin (predictions)

Somewhere on the long trail from India Gypsies adopted the mysterious old tarot cards and, handing down explanations of the strange pictures and symbols from mother to daughter, made them their own Gypsy tarot fortune telling cards. Tarot cards are known to have been used since the fifteenth century. They have been so differently interpreted that their true meaning can only be guessed and many interesting theories and speculations arise concerning their origin. But they seem always to have been used for making predictions and famous people, including Napoleon, consulted the tarot before making major decisions.

Each card in the Gypsy tarot has a specific meaning, influenced to some extent by those placed next to it. Predictions are made by 'reading' the meanings of selected cards in their relation to each other. Over the centuries our pack of fifty-two playing cards evolved from the tarot's seventy-two. Cups became hearts, platters diamonds, swords spades, and wands clubs. The ancestors of our court cards can also be recognized among the forty fantastic picture cards.

Gypsy women still tell fortunes today with the familiar modern pack. They call this activity 'durrikin'. Once you too have mastered the meaning of each card you are ready to try out your ability to predict the future.

To make predictions you need:
a pack of ordinary playing cards and a table (Gypsy Tarot cards can still be bought, but they are rare and expensive)

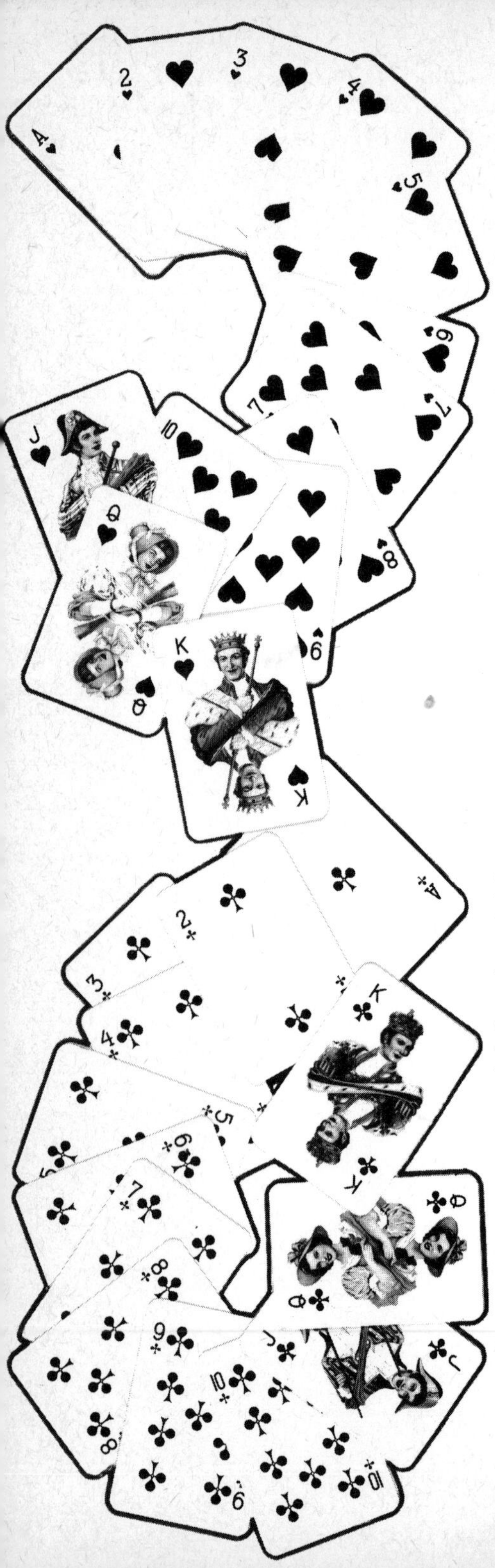

Memorize the meaning of each card.

Hearts stand for joy, home and fulfilment. Clubs mean justice, order and strength of mind. Diamonds represent money and creative ability and spades are the obstacles that must be overcome.

Hearts

Ace – a love affair
Two – broken romance
Three – pleasure and frivolity
Four – a good friend for life
Five – a change of surroundings
Six – you are too generous
Seven – joy through sorrow
Eight – a flirtation
Nine – wishes fulfilled
Ten – a wealthy visitor
Jack – a close friend is not to be trusted
Queen – a devoted wife
King – a handsome husband, quick tempered but generous

Clubs

Ace – success in business
Two – a reprimand for slackness
Three – payment for good work
Four – beware of spoken promises
Five – patient waiting rewarded
Six – hidden potential
Seven – ambitions can be realised but beware of dalliance
Eight – do not gamble or ask for a loan
Nine – good business prospects
Ten – illness averted
Jack – a sincere friend
Queen – a dependable woman
King – a loyal friend, husband and father, a rock in the storm

Diamonds
Ace – expect a gift
Two – a tragic love affair
Three – good advice from a tall thin person
Four – victim of fraud
Five – honesty pays
Six – early marriage may end in failure
Seven – keep silent or harm may be done
Eight – happiness through a journey
Nine – a journey over the water
Ten – sudden wealth
Jack – a cunning and clever young man
Queen – a shallow and frivolous woman
King – a ruthless man

Spades
Ace – death and sorrow
Two – a long journey
Three – tears over a love affair
Four – temporary loss of health or money
Five – patience rewarded
Six – good luck after a serious setback
Seven – quarrels, tears and sorrow
Eight – hidden snags
Nine – perseverence over strife
Ten – hidden enemies
Jack – a deceitful young man
Queen – a widow
King – an ambitious man, could be an enemy

Take a card from the pack and place it in the centre of the table to represent the sitter. Then ask him to shuffle the pack to infuse it with his personality and state of mind.

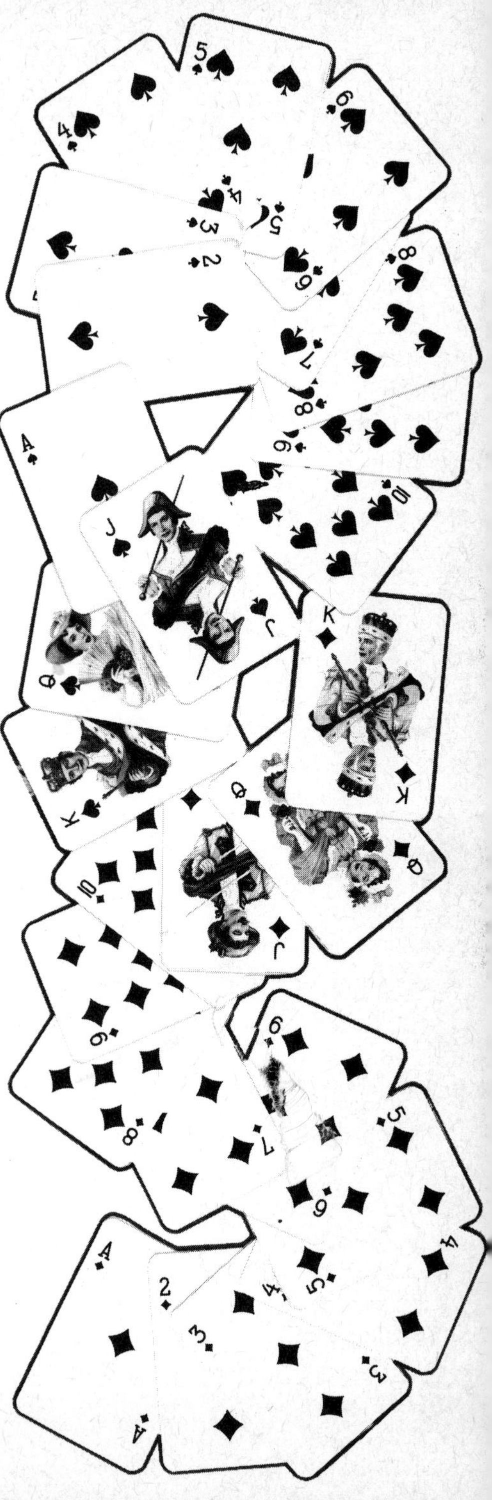

Force Majeure
Absolute Necessity
11.
La Force
Strength
16.
Jugement
Judgment
21.
Dissension
Disagreement
77.
Parfait Contentement
Absolute Harmony
48.
Amour
Love
2.
2.e Element. 1.e Creation
Eclaircissement
Enlightenment
5.
4 El.
Voyage
Travel
6 Cré.

Lay out twenty-seven cards, three at a time, in the order shown in the diagram. Chant the following as you do so:

> 'Three above you, three below you, three behind you, three before you, three for your house and home, three for your hopes and fears, three for what you don't expect, three for what you do expect and three for what's sure to come.'

Starting at number one, turn up the cards and study each group of three to make your predictions.

Gypsy women have always read palms and still do so at fairs. In the old days they often took their mischievous chavies with them and many a client found his pocket empty after leaving the tent.

To read a palm, study the main character lines on the right hand. If your client is left handed, study the left one.

Strong clear lines are good; feathery and broken ones mean periods of change and disorder; and chain-like lines mean that the client has worked, or must work hard to attain the quality.

The fate line is different; it is not a character line but predicts the future by showing what is likely to happen.

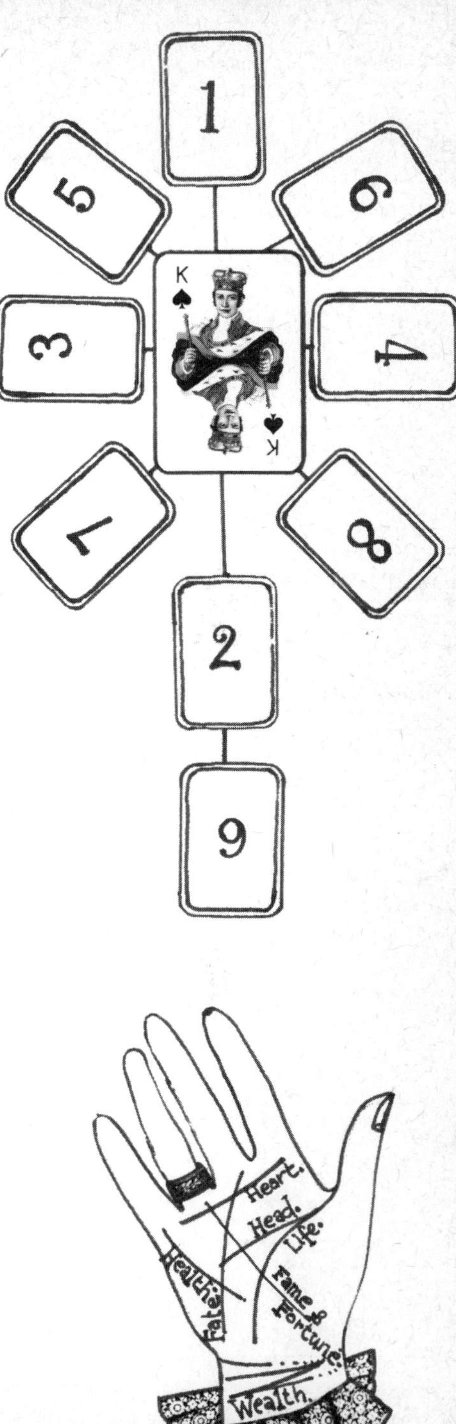

Lavender bottles

Sixty years ago a London Gypsy could still be heard singing her version of a very old street cry:

'Won't you buy my bright blooming lavender
Sixteen blue branches a penny
Now's the time to scent your pocket handkerchief
Pretty ladies
Sixteen blue branches a penny.

Fill your drawers with bright blue lavender
Sixteen blue branches a penny
Scent your silks your satins and your velvets
Pretty ladies
Sixteen blue branches a penny.'

Gypsies also made delightful little lavender bottles by tying up small bunches, bending the stalks to enclose the flower heads, and weaving through them with narrow silk ribbon. These they sold to the 'pretty ladies' to slip amongst their clothes in closets and drawers.

To make a lavender bottle you need:
seventeen long stalks of freshly picked lavender
1 metre (or 40 in) length of 50 mm (or $\frac{1}{4}$ in) wide baby ribbon
60 cm (or 2 ft) length of sewing cotton
a pair of scissors
two pins

Take seventeen long stalks of freshly picked lavender and start work immediately, before they become dry and brittle.

Tie them together with cotton just below the flower heads.

Bend up the stalks, one at a time, to form a cage round the flower heads.

Tie the stalks together again with cotton just above the flower heads. This should make a cage-like 'bottle' containing the flowers about 9 cm ($3\frac{1}{2}$ in) tall.

Cut a piece of baby ribbon about 72 cm (or 29 in) long. Secure it at the base of the bottle with a pin and weave it through the cage, in and out and round and round until you reach the top.

Secure the end with another pin. Trim off any surplus ribbon.

Wind the remaining piece of ribbon over the cotton and pin-head and tie it in a pretty bow.

Trim off the long stalk ends above the bow and the lavender bottle is complete.

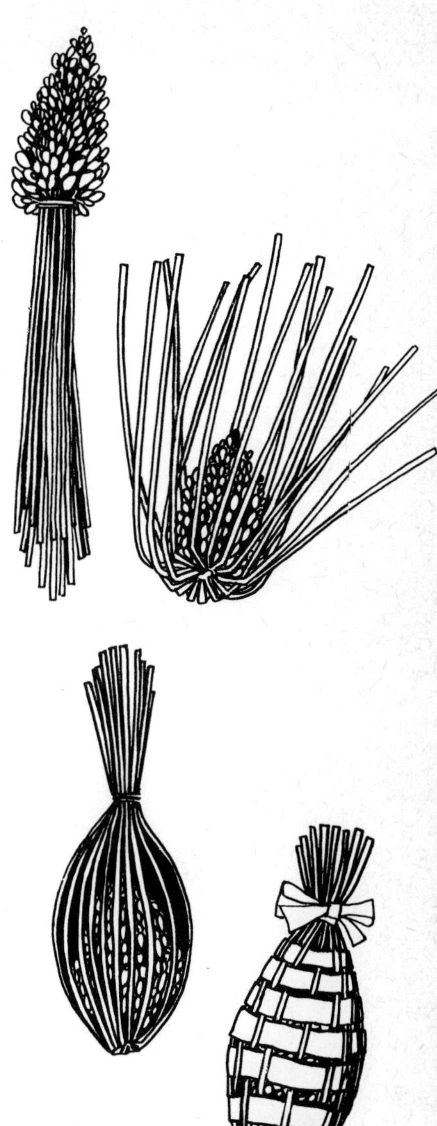

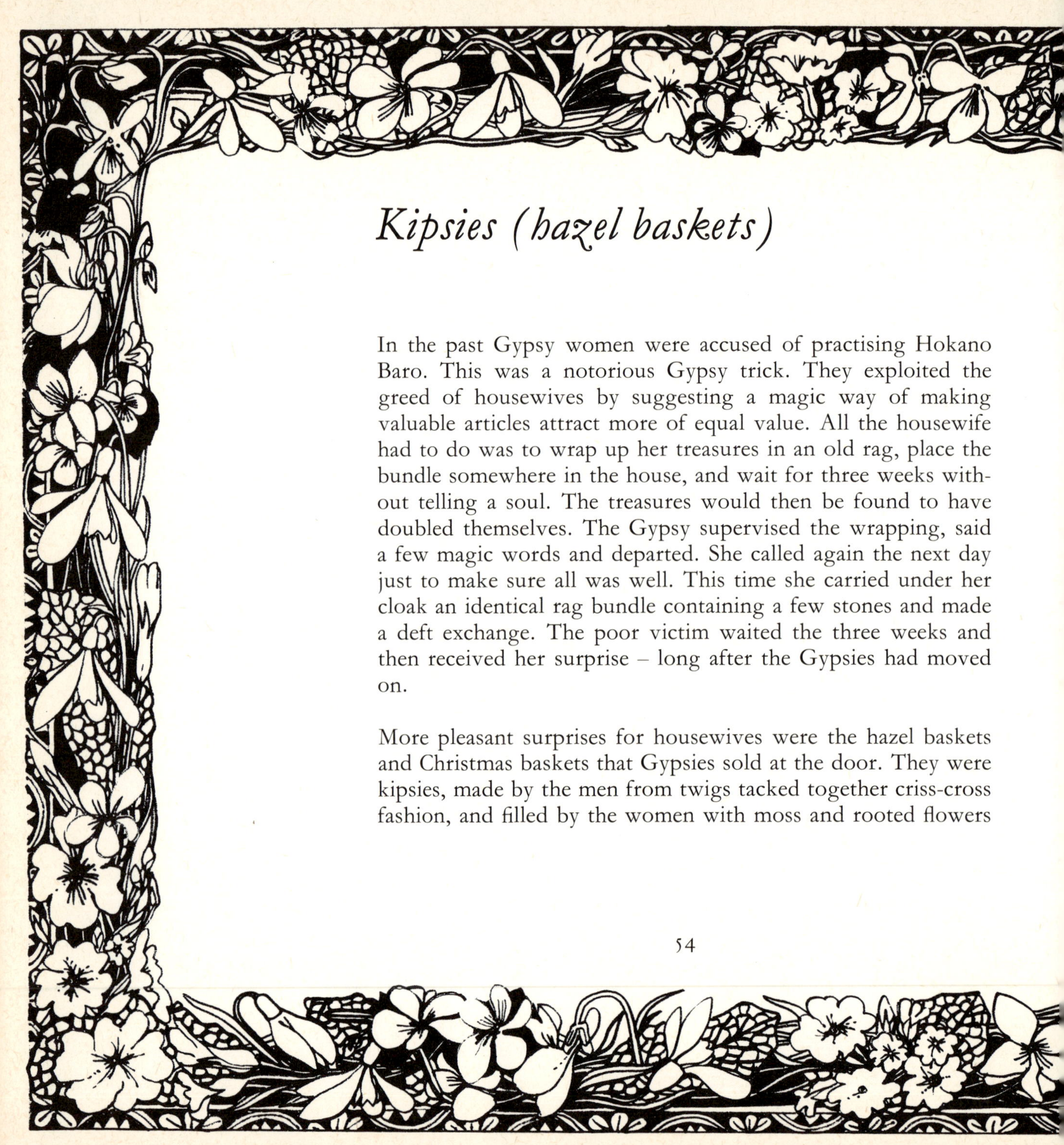

Kipsies (hazel baskets)

In the past Gypsy women were accused of practising Hokano Baro. This was a notorious Gypsy trick. They exploited the greed of housewives by suggesting a magic way of making valuable articles attract more of equal value. All the housewife had to do was to wrap up her treasures in an old rag, place the bundle somewhere in the house, and wait for three weeks without telling a soul. The treasures would then be found to have doubled themselves. The Gypsy supervised the wrapping, said a few magic words and departed. She called again the next day just to make sure all was well. This time she carried under her cloak an identical rag bundle containing a few stones and made a deft exchange. The poor victim waited the three weeks and then received her surprise – long after the Gypsies had moved on.

More pleasant surprises for housewives were the hazel baskets and Christmas baskets that Gypsies sold at the door. They were kipsies, made by the men from twigs tacked together criss-cross fashion, and filled by the women with moss and rooted flowers

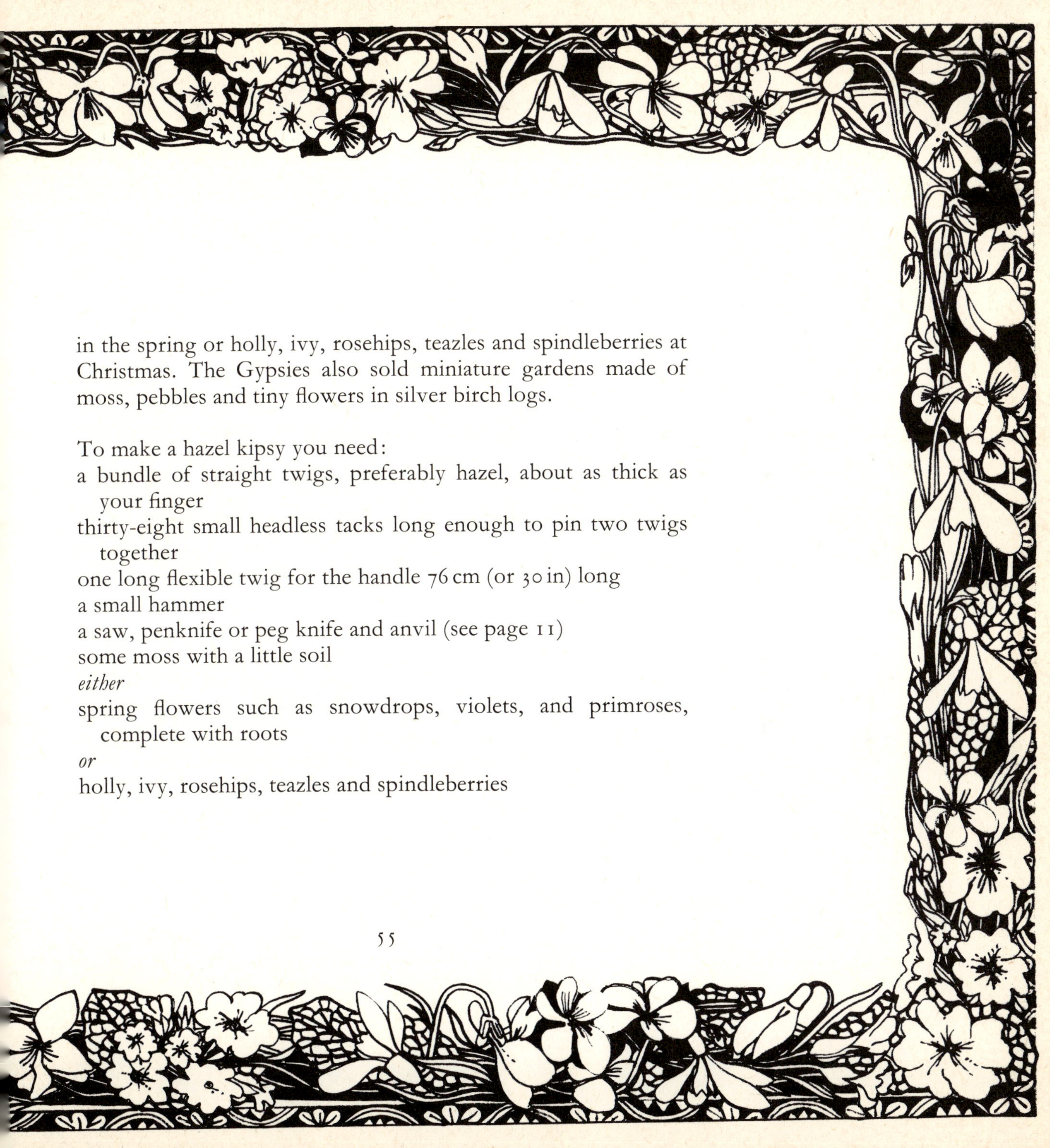

in the spring or holly, ivy, rosehips, teazles and spindleberries at Christmas. The Gypsies also sold miniature gardens made of moss, pebbles and tiny flowers in silver birch logs.

To make a hazel kipsy you need:

a bundle of straight twigs, preferably hazel, about as thick as your finger

thirty-eight small headless tacks long enough to pin two twigs together

one long flexible twig for the handle 76 cm (or 30 in) long

a small hammer

a saw, penknife or peg knife and anvil (see page 11)

some moss with a little soil

either

spring flowers such as snowdrops, violets, and primroses, complete with roots

or

holly, ivy, rosehips, teazles and spindleberries

Gather a bunch of attractive twigs of equal thickness, preferably hazel.

Use the saw, penknife or peg knife and anvil to cut up the twigs into the following lengths:
four twigs 12 cm (or $4\frac{3}{4}$ in)
four twigs 14 cm (or $5\frac{1}{2}$ in)
four twigs 16 cm (or $6\frac{1}{4}$ in)
four twigs 18 cm (or 7 in)
four twigs 20 cm (or $7\frac{3}{4}$ in)

Tack the twigs together to make five square frames with cross-over corners as shown in the drawing.

Tack the second largest frame onto the largest one as shown. Then tack on the last three frames in the same way, using them in decreasing order of size.

Turn the basket over so that the smallest frame becomes the base. Tack the long flexible twig securely to each side for the handle. The long handle is intentional so that the kipsy may be used as a hanging basket if you wish.

Put a few crossed twigs in the bottom, then fill the basket with moss with some soil attached. Plant it with rooted spring flowers, watering them well. Alternatively, decorate it with leaves and berries for a Christmas basket.

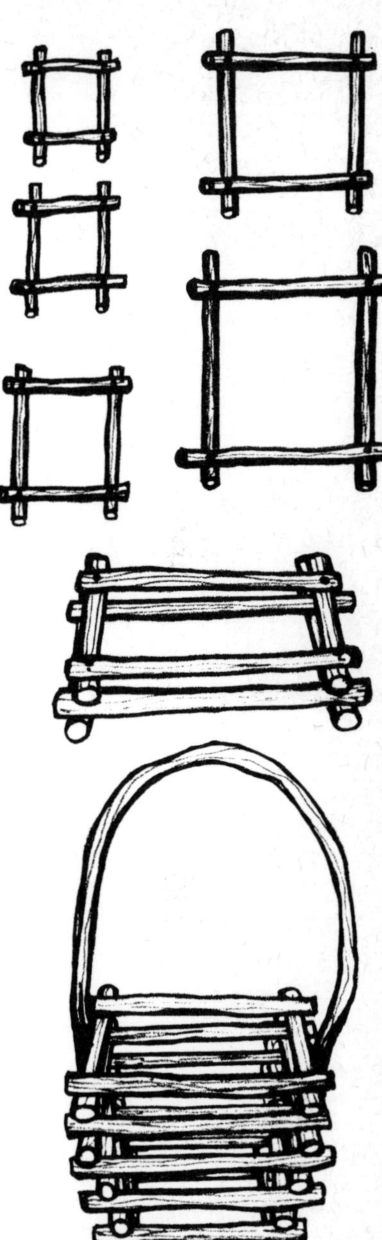

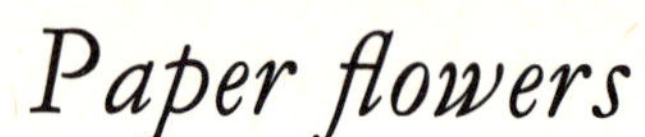

Paper flowers

A Gypsy never liked to die in his vardo. When he felt his days were numbered he moved out into a tent. After his death his crockery was smashed and buried and the wagon and all his worldly goods – except his jewelry and money – were burned. Many Gypsies were buried secretly in the woods in coffins made from hollow oak lined with ferns. They were dressed in their best clothes and often buried with their sweggler in one hand and an ounce of tobacco and a box of matches in the other. Singing and dancing accompanied the funeral. Other Gypsies were given a church burial and their relatives came to decorate the grave with candles and paper flowers.

Paper flowers were also made to sell. The best known Gypsy paper flower is the strange spidery bloom still sold in parts of Britain and France. Pink and orange roses were also made and, as an added refinement, dipped for an instant in melted wax. This enhanced their appearance and prevented them from being damaged by wind and weather.

To make paper flowers you need:
crêpe paper in various colours
pointed scissors
thin wire such as fuse wire or florist's wire
a few wax candles
some evergreen sprays of leaves

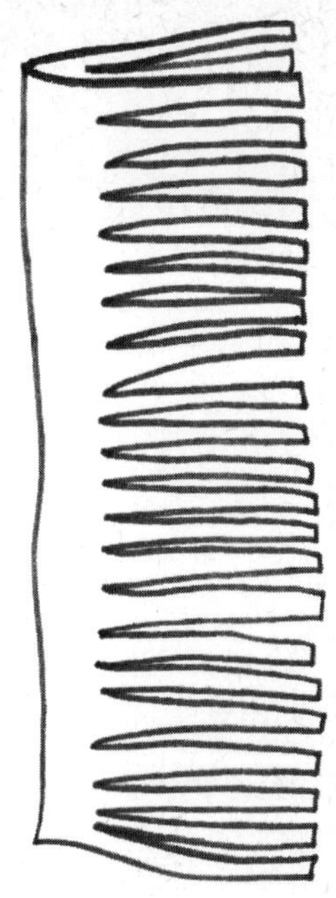

Take a small scrap of crêpe paper and pull it in two opposite directions. You will find that it stretches readily one way, but remains taut when pulled the other way. This quality is very useful in flower making.

To make the exotic flowers sold by Gypsies at fairs in France and Spain, cut a piece of crêpe paper 20 cm (or 8 in) wide and 50 cm (or 20 in) long, making sure that the paper stretches widthways.

Fold it in half, long sides together. Cut the doubled strip into a fringe, making the cuts about 1.5 cm (or $\frac{1}{2}$ in) apart and 8 cm (or $3\frac{1}{4}$ in) long.

Hold the base of the top double strand of the fringe firmly between your left forefinger and thumb with the thumb uppermost.

Hold the wide open scissors in your right hand and, using one blade only, score a central line down the underside of the strand with the scissor point. Press the point up against the paper and your right thumb.

As you score the strand pull it gently but firmly towards you to make the paper stretch and coil. Do not tear it or cut right through it.

Work down the whole fringe scoring and stretching each double strand in the same way.

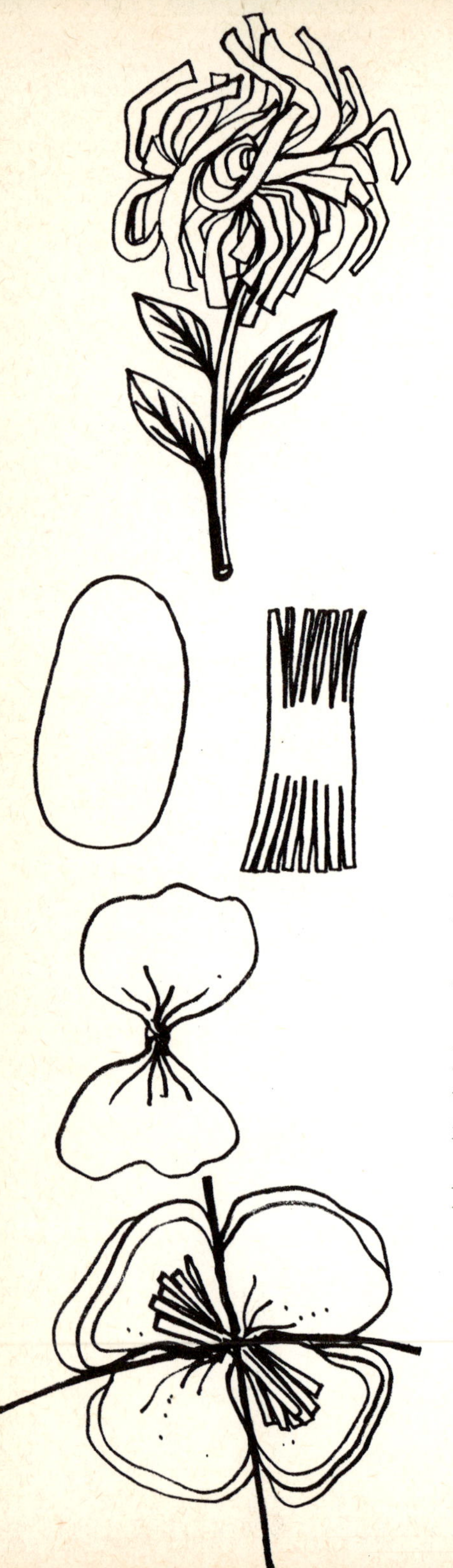

When this is done, roll up the fringe allowing the crinkly fronds to cascade all round.

Pinch the base and twist a short length of thin wire round it. Use this to attach the flower head to an evergreen sprig. Dark shiny leaves look attractive with these strange blooms.

Gypsies also sold many hundreds of pink and yellow paper roses. To make a convincing rose cut a strip of crêpe paper 10 cm (or 4 in) wide and 30 cm (or 12 in) long. This time make sure that the paper stretches lengthways.

Cut up the strip into six pieces each 5 × 10 cm (or 2 × 4 in). Take five of these and cut gentle curves to round off all the corners. Then take the sixth piece and cut a deep fringe along both the top and bottom (see drawings).

Hold the open scissors in your right hand as before and stroke all the curved edges back across the blade.

Twist each piece together in the middle to give it a waist.

Lay the pieces one on top of the other, criss-cross fashion, with the fringed piece on top. Place two strands of wire on top of this in the shape of an X, as shown in the diagram.

Bend the wires down between the papers to the underside and

twist them tightly together, bunching up the paper to form petals.

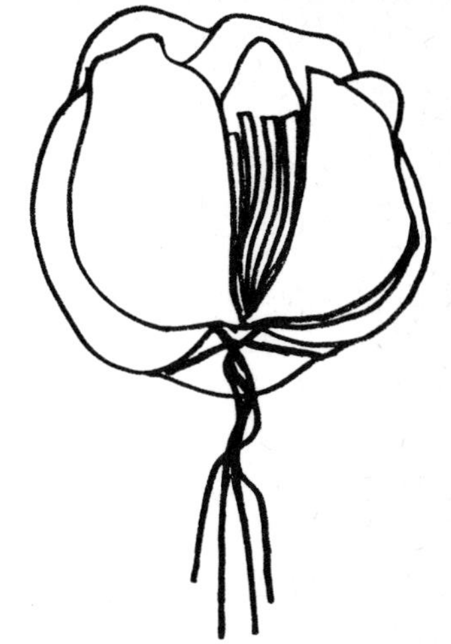

Taking full advantage of the stretchy nature of the paper, pull and pinch the petals until you have sculpted the flower head into a rose. It is very helpful to have a real rose or at least a picture of one by your side for reference.

When it is as perfect as you can make it, wire the rose onto an evergreen spray.

Roses were dipped in wax to make them waterproof. As they were hawked round in winter when real ones were in short supply, the wax afforded protection from rain and snow. It gives the flowers a deceptively delicate semi-transparent appearance and greatly enhances them.

To wax roses you need:
a small old saucepan
four broken white kitchen candles or a handful of clean stumps
some completed paper rose heads
a clean newspaper

Put the broken candles into the pan and heat them gently until they melt. Lift out the wicks with a fork and then dip each rose head into the hot wax for a second, holding it by its wire. Lay the roses lightly on the newspaper to dry.